LITERATURE AND CRITICAL THINKING

Art Projects • Bulletin Boards • Plot Summaries
Skill Building Activities • Independent Thinking

Written by: Patty Carratello
Illustrated by: Theresa Wright and Linda Smythe

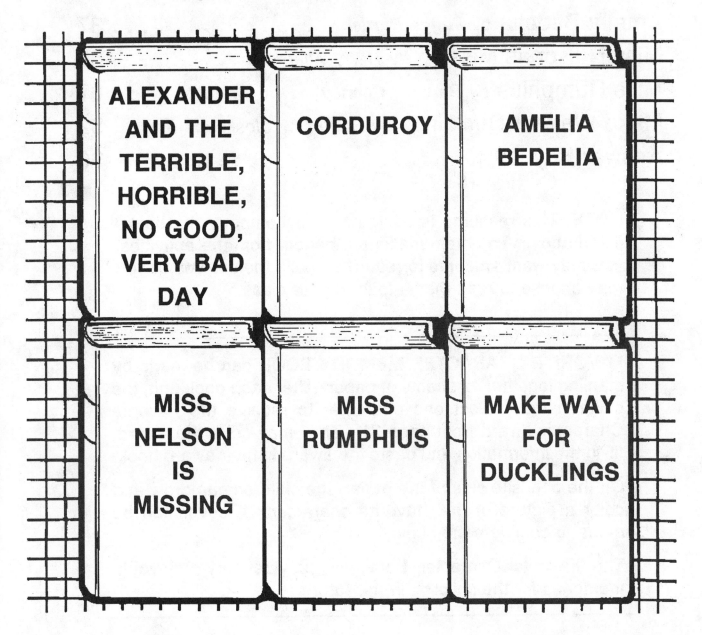

ALEXANDER AND THE TERRIBLE, HORRIBLE, NO GOOD, VERY BAD DAY

CORDUROY

AMELIA BEDELIA

MISS NELSON IS MISSING

MISS RUMPHIUS

MAKE WAY FOR DUCKLINGS

Teacher Created Materials, Inc.
P. O. Box 1214
Huntington Beach, CA 92649
© *Teacher Created Materials, Inc. 1988*
Made in U.S.A.

© *Teacher Created Materials, Inc. 1988*   ISBN 1-55734-357-8   *#357 Literature and Critical Thinking Book 3*

TABLE OF CONTENTS

NOTE: This resource is designed to accompany the books listed above. To obtain maximum benefit from the activities, you may want students to read the books themselves or you may choose to read them aloud to your class.

FAVORITE CHARACTER MEMORY BOOK can be made by stapling together 12 sheets of paper. After each book unit, the children may select one character to receive the Favorite Character Award from page 21. They may color the award, fill in the information and paste the award in their award book.

On the opposite side of the paper, the children can draw and color a picture of their favorite character. A cover can be made to complete the book.

The Favorite Character Book will provide very enjoyable memories for the children in the future.

INTRODUCTION

LITERATURE AND CRITICAL THINKING

It is possible for all children at varying developmental levels to engage in a discovery process which clarifies thinking, increases knowledge, and deepens their understanding of human issues and social values. This activities book, based on Bloom's *Taxonomy of Skills in the Cognitive Domain*, provides teachers a resource to maximize this process, using distinguished children's literature as a vehicle.

The authors suggest the following options in using this book:

OPTION 1: The teacher may select a single activity for the entire class.

OPTION 2: The teacher may select different activities for single students or small groups of students.

OPTION 3: The student may select the level at which he or she wishes to work, once the teacher explains what is available.

The stories in this book follow the same format, so that each level of thinking skills is approached as follows:

KNOWLEDGE

This level provides the child with an opportunity to recall fundamental facts and information about the story. Success at this level will be evidenced by the child's ability to:

• Match character names with pictures of the characters.
• Identify the main characters in a crossword puzzle.
• Match statements with the characters who said them.
• List the main characteristics of one of the main characters in a WANTED poster.
• Arrange scrambled story pictures in sequential order.
• Arrange scrambled story sentences in sequential order.
• Recall details about the setting by creating a picture of where a part of the story took place.

COMPREHENSION

This level provides the child with an opportunity to demonstrate a basic understanding of the story. Success at this level will be evidenced by the child's ability to:

• Interpret pictures of scenes from the story.
• Explain selected ideas or parts from the story in his or her own words.

COMPREHENSION (Continued)

- Draw a picture showing what happened before and after a passage or illustration found in the book.
- Write a sentence explaining what happened before and after a passage or illustration found in the book.
- Predict what *could* happen next in the story before the reading of the entire book is completed.
- Construct a pictorial time line which summarizes what happens in the story.
- Explain how the main character felt at the beginning, middle, and/or end of the story.

APPLICATION

This level provides the child with an opportunity to use information from the story in a new way. Success at this level will be evidenced by the child's ability to:

- Classify the characters as human, animal, or thing.
- Transfer a main character to a new setting.
- Make finger puppets and act out a part of the story.
- Select a meal that one of the main characters would enjoy eating, plan a menu, and a method of serving it.
- Think of a situation that occurred to a character in the story and write about how he or she would have handled the situation differently.
- Give examples of people the child knows who have the same problems as the characters in the story.

ANALYSIS

This level provides the child with an opportunity to take parts of the story and examine these parts carefully in order to better understand the whole story. Success at this level will be evidenced by the child's ability to:

- Identify general characteristics (stated and/or implied) of the main characters.
- Distinguish what could happen from what couldn't happen in the story in real life.
- Select parts of the story that were funniest, saddest, happiest, and most unbelievable.
- Differentiate fact from opinion.
- Compare and/or contrast two of the main characters.
- Select an action of a main character that was exactly the same as something the child would have done.

SYNTHESIS

This level provides the child with an opportunity to put parts from the story together in a new way to form a new idea or product. Success at this level will be evidenced by the child's ability to:

- Create a story from just the title before the story is read (pre-story exercise).
- Write three new titles for the story that would give a good idea what it was about.
- Create a poster to advertise the story so people will want to read it.
- Create a new product related to the story.
- Restructure the roles of the main characters to create new outcomes in the story.
- Compose and perform a dialogue or monologue that will communicate the thoughts of the main character(s) at a given point in the story.
- Imagine that he or she is one of the main characters and write a diary account of daily thoughts and activities.
- Create an original character and tell how the character would fit into the story.
- Write the lyrics and music to a song that one of the main characters would sing if he/she/it became a rock star — and perform it.

EVALUATION

This level provides the child with an opportunity to form and present an opinion backed up by sound reasoning. Success at the level will be evidenced by the child's ability to:

- Decide which character in the selection he or she would most like to spend a day with and why.
- Judge whether or not a character should have acted in a particular way and why.
- Decide if the story really could have happened and justify reasons for the decision.
- Consider how this story can help the child in his or her own life.
- Appraise the value of the story.
- Compare this story with another one the child has read.
- Write a recommendation as to why the books should be read or not.

In addition to the activities just outlined, a class project and a small groups project will be included for each story.

Alexander and the Terrible, Horrible, No Good, Very Bad Day

by Judith Viorst

Alexander got out of bed one morning, discovered gum in his hair, slipped on his skateboard, dropped his sweater in a sink with running water, and knew it would be a terrible, horrible, no good, very bad day.

And, he was right.

He didn't get a toy in his cereal box and his brothers did. He didn't get a window seat in the carpool and the others did. His best friend was not loyal, his invisible castle picture was unappreciated, he sang too loudly, he had no dessert in his lunch, so he decided Australia would be better than where he was.

It might have been.

He had a cavity, got covered with mud, fought with his brother, had to settle for plain white tennis shoes, tornadoed his father's office, and even had to eat lima beans and watch kissing on TV.

Imagine!

And as his day came to a close, he got soap in his eyes, lost a marble down the drain, and had to wear his hated railroad pajamas to bed and he had no cat to keep him company.

But his mother told him some days are like that - even in Australia!

OH, NO!

Many things went wrong for Alexander one day.

Draw pictures of two things that went wrong.

This happened to Alexander one day.

This happened to Alexander one day.

OH, NO!

Fill in the blanks of the problems Alexander has in the story. The words to help you are next to Alexander's picture.

WANTED

Problems for Alexander

cavity
cereal
white
skateboard
lima
friend

sixteen
gum
dessert
mud
cat
books

These terrible, horrible, no good, very bad things happened to me today.

1. There was g_____ in my hair.

2. I tripped on my s_____.

3. I had no toy in my breakfast c_____.

4. I was not Paul's best f_____.

5. My mother did not pack d_____ in my lunch.

6. The dentist found a c_____ in my tooth.

7. I fell in the m_____.

8. I had to buy plain, w_____ tennis shoes.

9. I had l_____ beans for dinner.

10. The c_____ did not want to sleep with me.

8

NEW SHOES!

Color the tennis shoes the way Alexander wished his new shoes would look.

THE PERFECT PLACE!

Here are travel stickers to four places in the world. Color and cut out the place Alexander thinks will be perfect for him. Paste this sticker on his travel bag on page 11.

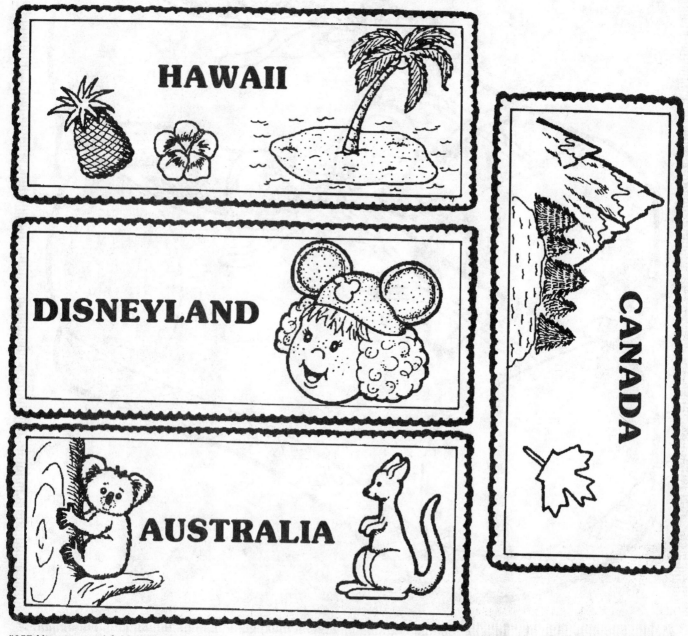

10

THE PERFECT PLACE!

1. Color all of the bag except the rectangle.
2. Paste the place sticker from page 10 on the bag.
3. Cut out the travel bag.

Alexander is ready to go!

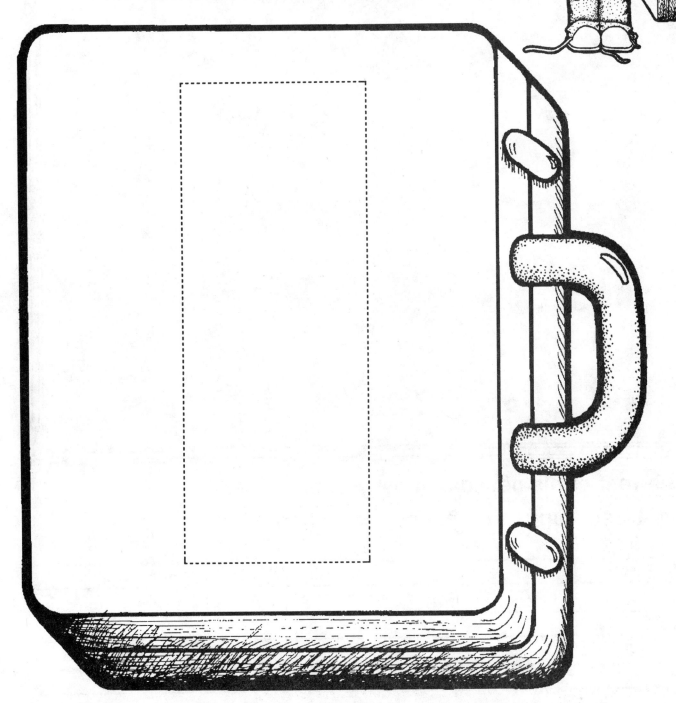

A NEW DAY

Alexander's terrible, horrible, no good, very bad day is over. Today is a new day.

Draw a picture of the first thing that happens to him on this new day.

Is the rest of his new day mostly good or bad?_____

Write three things that happened to him on this new day.

1._____

_____

2._____

_____

3._____

12

A DIFFERENT WAY

Cut out these strips. Color the face on each strip the correct color. You will need the strips for the next page. Be sure to read them first with your teacher.

 # 1. I would be mad.

(red)

 # 2. I would cry.

(blue)

 # 3. I would laugh.

(yellow)

 # 4. I would yell and scream.

(green)

 # 5. I would do something about it.

(orange)

 # 6. I would do nothing.

(purple)

 # 7. I would do just what Alexander did.

(pink)

A DIFFERENT WAY

Your teacher will read Alexander's problems on this page. Choose an answer strip that shows what you might do for each problem. Write the number of the strip next to the problem. (You may use one strip more than once.) When the teacher asks the class for their answers, the whole class will hold up their colored strips at the same time.

① I have gum all over my hair.   #_____

② I slipped on my skateboard.   #_____

③ Everyone got a cereal prize except me.   #_____

④ The teacher was not pleased with my picture. #_____

⑤ I didn't get dessert in my lunch.   #_____

⑥ I was the only one with a cavity.   #_____

⑦ I had to eat lima beans.   #_____

⑧ I saw kissing on T.V.   #_____

⑨ I had to wear pajamas I didn't like.   #_____

⑩ My cat wouldn't sleep with me.   #_____

☆ Could you answer every problem
   with a strip?_____

☆ If not, which problems could you
   not find a strip for?_____

☆ Tell your new answer(s) to the class

MY PROBLEMS, TOO!

Write your name under each of Alexander's problems that **could** happen to you.

1. I got gum in my hair.

   _____

2. I dropped my sweater in a sink with water.

   _____

3. I didn't get to sit by the window in the car.

   _____

4. I sang too loudly.

   _____

5. My best friend said he didn't like me best.

   _____

6. I fell in mud and cried.

   _____

7. I hit my brother (or sister) and Mom (or Dad) yelled at me.

   _____

8. I got soap in my eyes.

   _____

On the back of this paper, draw one of these things happening to you!

PROBLEMS IN PICTURES

Draw your ideas in these boxes.

This is Alexander's **biggest** problem.

This is Alexander's **smallest** problem.

This is Alexander's **funniest** problem.

This is the problem Alexander has that I have the most.

16

ALEXANDER DOLL

Page 1

1. Color Alexander

2. Cut him out

There are three pages for this project.

Teacher, reproduce pages 1 and 2 on heavy paper.

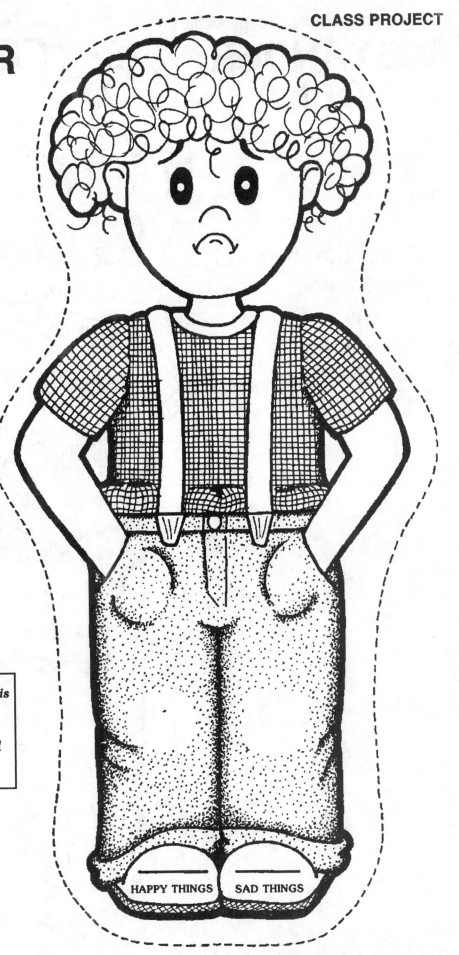

HAPPY THINGS   SAD THINGS

ALEXANDER DOLL

Page 2

1. Color the back of Alexander.

2. Cut him out.

18

ALEXANDER DOLL

Page 3

To put Alexander together:

1. Put Alexander's back and front together.
2. Staple 3/4 of the way around him.
3. Stuff him with cotton balls or shredded paper.
4. Staple the rest of him closed.

Are your days filled with good or bad things?   Let your Alexander Doll help you find out!

Color and cut out the happy and sad faces below. Now you are ready for a day with Alexander! Every time something good happens, glue or tape a happy face on Alexander's shirt or pants. Every time something bad happens, glue or tape on a sad face. At the end of the day, count how many happy and sad faces you have. Write the number on Alexander's tennis shoes.

READ IT!

You have just finished reading *Alexander and the Terrible, Horrible, No Good, Very Bad Day.*

1. Did you like the story? _____
   Why? _____
   _____
   _____
   _____
   _____

2. Do you know anyone who would like to read this book?___
   Who? (Write names on lines below)

   ① _____
   ② _____
   ③ _____
   ④ _____
   ⑤ _____

3. Would you read this book again? _____
   Why? _____
   _____
   _____
   _____

I LIKE...

Which one of the characters in the story do you like best? _____

Why? _____

_____

Which of the characters in the story do you like least? _____

_____

Why? _____

_____

Make an award for your favorite character.
Fill in the blanks on the ribbon. Color the
ribbon and cut it out. Put the
ribbon in your Favorite Character
memory book.

(See page 2)

character's name →

your name →

a few words about
your character →

book and author →

**Favorite
Character Award**
presented to

_____

by

_____

because you are

_____

_____

Author: Book:

_____   _____

_____   _____

Corduroy

by Don Freeman

A little bear named Corduroy waited in a toy store, eager to be purchased. Love at first sight made a young girl want to buy him, but her mother said no, because she had already spent too much money. She also felt Corduroy's missing button made him look like he wasn't new.

Corduroy hadn't realized a button had been missing from his overalls. As he set out that night to find the lost button in the department store, he encountered a number of adventures and mishaps until a night watchman returned him to the toy shelf.

The next day, the same girl returned to buy Corduroy with her piggy bank money. Lisa cuddled Corduroy on the way home, making him feel comfortable, and then sewed on a new button. They had each found a friend.

22

COLOR ME!

Color Corduroy's overalls the same color they were in the story.
Then, color Corduroy!

WHO SAID THAT?

Cut out these word "bubbles" and paste them next to the characters who said them on page 25.

"Oh, Mommy! There's the very bear I've always wanted."

"I didn't know I'd lost a button."

"Hello! How did you get upstairs?"

"Not today, dear. I've spent too much already. Besides, he doesn't look new."

"I like you the way you are, but you'll be more comfortable with your shoulder strap fastened."

"You must be a friend. I've always wanted a friend."

24

WHO SAID THAT?

Color the pictures.

Paste the word bubbles from page 24 in the blank bubbles next to the characters who said them.

LOST!

1. Draw a picture of what Corduroy was looking for at night in the store.

2. Did he ever find the one he had lost? _____

3. What did Lisa do about what Corduroy lost? _____

_____

_____

_____

26

WHAT, WHERE, AND WHEN?

What was Corduroy doing when he said these things? Cut out your answer pictures from page 28. Paste the pictures above the words they belong with. Then, cut out each work-picture box. Paste the boxes on a piece of construction paper in story order.

"I guess I've always wanted to live in a palace."

"I know I've always wanted a home."

"I've always wanted a friend."

"I've always wanted to sleep in a bed."

"I think I've always wanted to climb a mountain."

WHAT, WHERE, AND WHEN?

Color these pictures from the story. Cut them out. Paste the pictures above the words they belong with on page 27.

28

WHAT IS THIS?

Read this list. Decide what is human, animal, or thing. Write each word on the list under the right picture.

LIST

Overalls	*Night Watchman*
Lisa	*Button*
Mattress	*Lisa's Mother*
Flashlight	*Piggy bank*
Saleslady	*Corduroy*

HUMAN	ANIMAL	THING
		THE Book *by the: author*

OUR PERFECT DAY

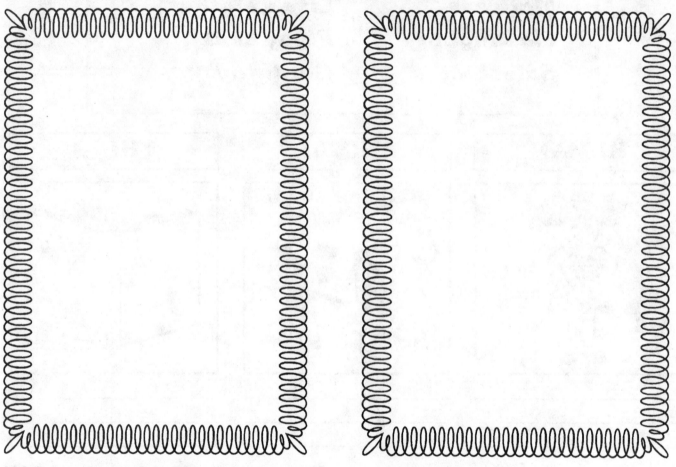

1. Use what you know about Lisa and Corduroy to plan a perfect day for them! Where would they go? What would they do?

2. Draw pictures of two things they would do on their perfect day.

Lisa and Corduroy's Perfect Day

Write more things you think they might like to do.

1._____

2._____

3._____

4._____

30

COULD THIS HAPPEN?

Here is a list of things that happen in the story. Color the bears next to the sentences that could **really** happen.

1. A toy bear is in a toy store.

2. A child's mother tells her she can't have a toy.

3. A toy bear talks.

4. A toy bear gets on and rides the escalator by himself.

5. A toy bear pulls a button off a mattress.

6. A night watchman tries to find out what made a loud crash in a store.

7. A girl spends the money she has saved for a toy bear.

8. A girl and a toy bear talk to each other.

 #357 Literature and Critical Thinking Book 3

I WOULD DO THE SAME THING!

Color these pictures. Write your name under each picture if it is something you would do, too.

32

CORDUROY SEWING CARD

1. Color Corduroy.

2. Push or punch out the dots all around Corduroy, in the button, and in the button space.

3. Start at the "start" arrow dot and push your yarn up through the dot. Continue sewing up and down all around Corduroy.

4. Cut out the button and sew it onto Corduroy's strap.

5. Tape the end of the yarn to the back of the card.

Teacher Note: Use heavy weight paper to reproduce Corduroy. Tape the end of a 30 inch piece of yarn for each child, making a shoelace-like end. Be sure child starts yarn from the back.

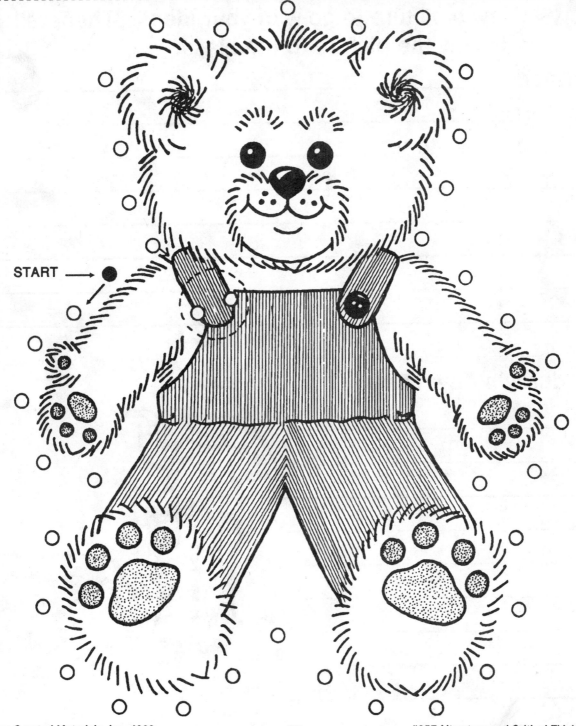

START →

CORDUROY'S ADVENTURE!

1. Suppose the night watchman did not find Corduroy? What could happen to Corduroy? Would he ever be found? Would he have adventures? Would he ever meet Lisa?

2. Work with a partner. Imagine what could happen to Corduroy. Choose one or two of your ideas and write a new story. Draw a picture to go with your ideas. Then, tell your story and show the picture to the class.

Partner:_____

Partner:_____

Ideas for new story: _____

_____

_____

_____

_____

_____

_____

3. Corduroy's Adventure!

_____

_____

_____

_____

_____

_____

_____

_____

34

SEE ME!

Look at these three people. Circle the person you would like to have most for a friend. Color the pictures.

1. Why did you circle the one you did? _____

_____

2. Sometimes people like or do not like people because of the clothes they wear. All they see is the clothes - they don't see what the person is really like.

   Lisa liked Corduroy from the start. Why? _____

_____

_____

3. Lisa said to Corduroy, "I like you the way your are, but you'll be more comfortable with your shoulder strap fastened."

   What does that mean? _____

_____

4. Do you like Corduroy the way he is? _____ Why? _____

_____

I'VE ALWAYS WANTED

Corduroy has ideas about what he wants to do and have. Draw a picture of what you think he wants most.

Do you have ideas about what you want to do and have? Finish these sentences with what you want. Then draw a picture of what you want most.

1. I guess I've always wanted to live _____

   _____

2. I've always wanted to sleep in _____

   _____

3. I know I've always wanted _____

   _____

What I Want Most

Amelia Bedelia

by **Peggy Parish**

Amelia Bedelia was ready to start her first day of work for Mr. and Mrs. Rogers. Mrs. Rogers gave Amelia a list of things to do, and then headed out for the day with her husband.

Before reading the list, Amelia decided to make a surprise lemon-meringue pie for her new employers. She put it in the oven and then began to read her jobs. "Change the towels in the green bathroom," the first direction read. And Amelia, the literal reader, did. She created grand new designs using scissors and her creativity. She certainly did "change" the towels!

Her literal interpretations made for an interesting work day. She did things such as dust the furniture with dusting powder when told to dust. A clothesline full of light bulbs was the response to "Put out the lights when you finish in the living room." You can imagine what she did to a chicken when she was told to dress it!

Although quite angry at the mishaps Amelia's interpretations created, Mr. and Mrs. Rogers took one bite of Amelia's lemon-meringue pie and decided to let her stay.

However, they did give their ensuing directions with more clarity!

THE FIRST THING

Color the picture of what Amelia Bedelia does **first** in the story.

38

CHANGE THE TOWELS!

1. Amelia is told to change the towels in the green bathroom.

2. Color these towels the right color.

3. Use scissors to cut them out and change them the way Amelia does.

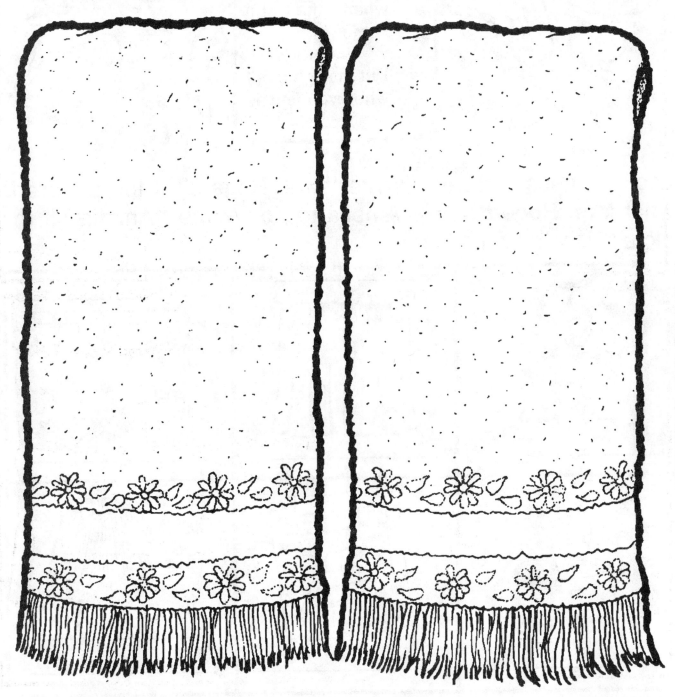

WORD FOR WORD

Read Mrs. Rogers' list.

Look at these pictures. Write "Mrs. Rogers" if the picture is what Mrs. Rogers wants Amelia to do. Write "Amelia" if the picture is what Amelia does.

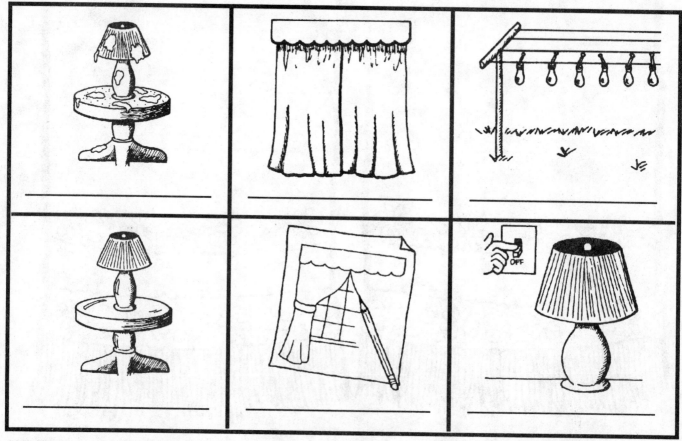

BECAUSE . . .

Draw a picture of the reason Mr. and Mrs. Rogers decided to keep Amelia working for them.

RHYMING NAMES

Amelia Bedelia has a rhyming name. The first name has the same **end** sound as the last name.

Match these two lists to make 10 rhyming names. Write the rhyming last name next to the first name it rhymes with.

AMELIA

BEDELIA

FIRST

1. Bill _____

2. Amy _____

3. David _____

4. Christopher _____

5. Ivan _____

6. Becky _____

7. Joe _____

8. Mary _____

9. Lisa _____

10. Nicky _____

LAST

Zecky

Histopher

Fisa

Kicky

Ramy

Parry

Twill

Ryvan

Hoe

Mavid

BILL

BECKY

Think of one more name that rhymes. Write it here.

_____

    42

HI, AMELIA!

Amelia has just come to **your** house to work! Make a list of 5 things you would like her to do. Be sure to make the directions **very** clear.

1. _____

   _____

   _____

   _____

2. _____

   _____

   _____

3. _____

   _____

   _____

4. _____

   _____

   _____

5. _____

   _____

Read your jobs to the class. Does your class think your directions are clear? _____

If not, how could you make changes? _____

_____

HA! HA! HA!

Draw a picture of the funniest thing you
think Amelia did.

hee   hee   hee   hee   hee   hee

ha   ha

ha   ha

ha   ha

ha   ha

ha   ha

ha   ha

hee   hee   hee   hee   hee   hee

DO WHAT YOU ARE TOLD!

Did Amelia do what she was told to do? _____
Perhaps Mrs. Rogers has learned to give Amelia better directions.

★ Circle the direction that tells Amelia **exactly** what to do.

1. Change the towels in the green bathroom.

   Replace the towels in the green bathroom with clean ones.

2. Dust the furniture.

   Wipe the dust from the furniture.

3. Close the drapes when the sun shines directly in the window.

   Draw the drapes when the sun comes in.

4. Turn the lights off when you finish in the living room.
   Put the lights out when you finish in the living room.

5. Dress the chicken.
   Get the chicken ready to cook.

BEST DRESSED CHICKEN

Mrs. Rogers did not give Amelia clear directions about dressing the chicken. Amelia dressed it the best she could.

You dress the chicken the best you can! Color and cut out the chicken. Color and cut out the clothes on the next two pages for your chicken.   Attach the clothes to your chicken with tabs and tape. You do not have to use all the clothes, just the ones you like. You may even want to create your own **original** clothing.

When you and your classmates have dressed your chickens, have a fashion show! You may even want to vote for the "Best Dressed Chicken!"

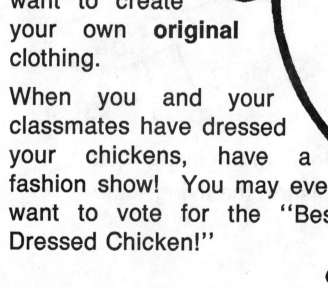
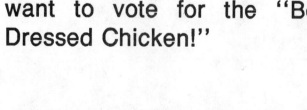

BEST DRESSED CHICKEN

1. Color and cut out all pieces.
2. Cut along dashed lines.
3. Dress your chicken!

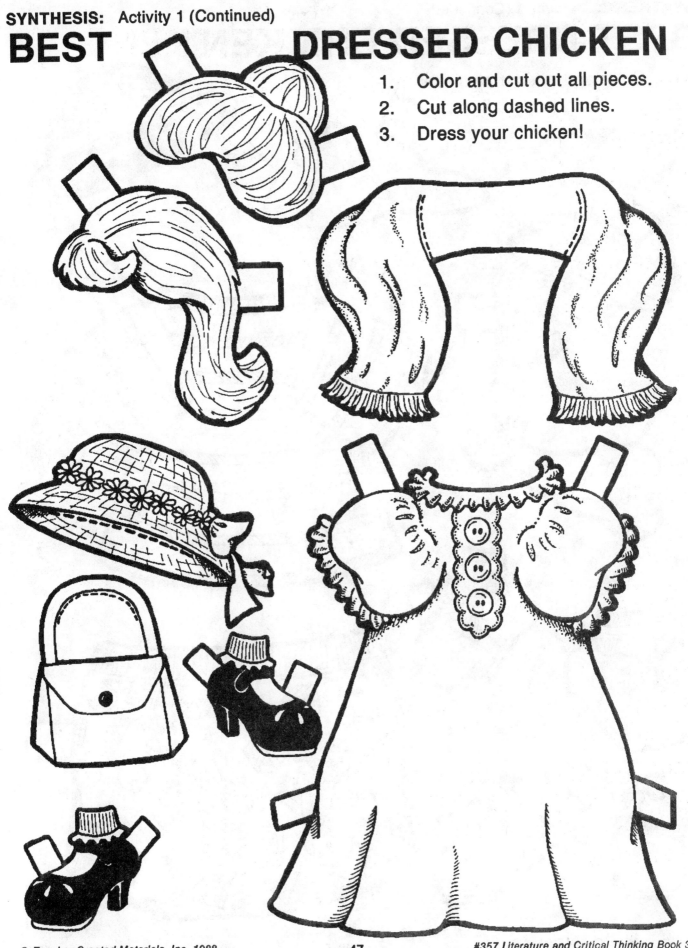

BEST DRESSED CHICKEN

1. Color and cut out all pieces.
2. Cut along dashed lines.
3. Dress your chicken!

48

DO WHAT?

1. Make a list of **three** things for Amelia to do that are **not** clearly explained.
2. Write directions that you are sure will make Amelia do what you **don't** want!

3. Under the directions, write what Amelia will do and what you want her to do.
4. Draw pictures of her work on separate paper.

★ Work in groups of 2 or 3. When you have finished, read your directions and show your pictures to the class.

1. Directions: _____

_____

Amelia will: _____

_____

We want her to: _____

_____

2. Directions: _____

_____

Amelia will: _____

_____

We want her to: _____

_____

3. Directions: _____

_____

Amelia will: _____

_____

We want her to: _____

_____

THE NEW JOB

Draw a large X over each picture of something Amelia should not have done.

Color each picture of something Amelia did that was right.

50

THE LETTER

You have just finished reading *Amelia Bedelia.*

Write a letter to a person you know. Tell him or her why you liked or didn't like the book. Also, explain why you think this person should or should not read the book.

_____
(date)

Dear

    I have just finished reading the book *Amelia Bedelia.* I _____
(liked/did not like)

this book because _____

_____

_____

_____

    I think you _____ read this book because
(should/should not)

_____

_____

_____

_____

Sincerely,

_____

Miss Nelson is Missing

by Harry Allard

Miss Nelson is the teacher of the worst-behaved class in the school. The students in Room 207 toss spitballs and paper airplanes, whisper and giggle, squirm and make faces, refuse to settle down or do lessons, and are rude during story hour. Miss Nelson decides to do something drastic.

She becomes Miss Viola Swamp, a mean witch of a woman who the students think is a substitute while their sweet Miss Nelson is "away." Miss Viola Swamp "whips" them into shape with a no-nonsense approach, and the former misbehavers do what she demands.

The students in Room 207 desperately miss their kind Miss Nelson. Miss Viola Swamp works them **so** hard and never reads them stories. The children fear that they might be stuck with Miss Viola Swamp forever.

However, Miss Nelson sheds her disguise and returns, to a thankful, happy, well-behaved group of students. They have, it seems, learned their lesson.

WHAT DID THEY DO?

Color the things the students did in Miss Nelson's class at the **beginning** of the story.

They whispered and giggled.

They always did their lessons.

They were quiet when Miss Nelson read stories.

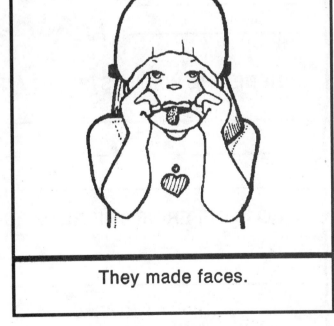

They made faces.

WANTED

Make a wanted poster for Miss Viola Swamp.

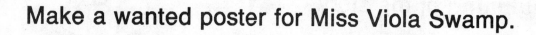

DESCRIPTION: _____

_____

_____

MISS VIOLA SWAMP

CRIME   REWARD

_____   _____

_____   _____

_____   _____

_____   _____

_____   _____

WHERE SHE WAS LAST SEEN AND WHAT SHE WAS DOING:

_____

_____

_____

WHO IS OFFERING THE REWARD FOR CAPTURE AND WHY:

_____

_____

_____

54

MISSING PERSON

1. What really happened to Miss Nelson?
2. Draw a picture of where she has been.

This is where Miss Nelson has been!

WHAT IS GOING ON HERE?

1. Explain what is happening in these pictures.
2. Color the pictures.

TELL US!

Page 1

This is a 3-page activity.

1. Choose one bad thing the students in Room 207 do. Write it here.

_____

_____

2. What would Miss Nelson say to them?

_____

_____

3. What would Miss Viola Swamp say to them? _____

_____

_____

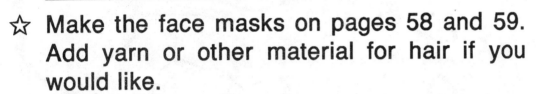

☆ Make the face masks on pages 58 and 59. Add yarn or other material for hair if you would like.

☆ Perform in front of the class. Tell your classmates what bad thing the students have done. Put on your Miss Nelson mask to tell the class what Miss Nelson would do. Put on your Miss Viola Swamp mask to tell the class what Miss Viola Swamp would do. Use the type of voice that you think each character might have. Have fun!

INSTRUCTIONS FOR MASKS ON PAGES 58 AND 59

1. Color mask.
2. Cut out eye and mouth holes.
3. Cut out mask. Cut nose along dotted line.
4. Stick several layers of tape on and behind holes for attaching mask. Then punch out holes and tie yarn through holes.

TELL US!

This is a 3-page activity.

Page 2

Cut Out

Cut Out

Cut Out

See instructions on page 57.

TELL US!

This Is a 3-page activity.

Page 3

Miss Viola Swamp

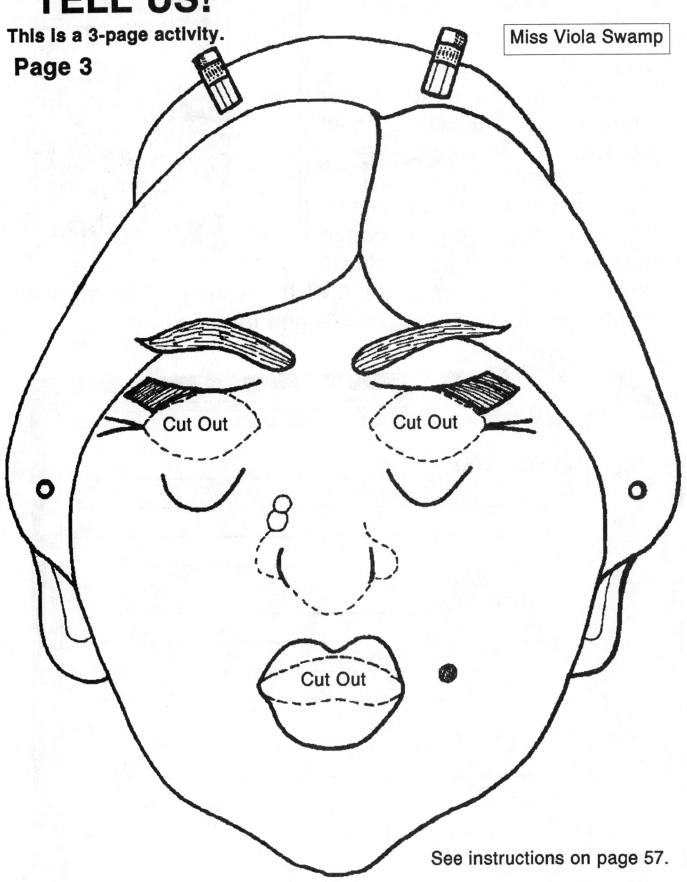

See instructions on page 57.

ROOM 207

☆ Miss Nelson has a class of misbehaving students.　She thinks of a plan to teach her students a lesson about behavior.

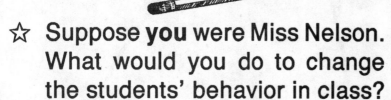

☆ Suppose **you** were Miss Nelson. What would you do to change the students' behavior in class? Work with a partner to think of three ideas.　Be sure to mention the behavior to be changed in each idea.

How to Change Bad Behavior

IDEA 1: _____

_____

_____

_____

IDEA 2: _____

_____

_____

_____

IDEA 3: _____

_____

_____

_____

by _____ and _____

BEHAVING OR MISBEHAVING

Decide which of these actions is behaving and which is misbehaving. Color the correct circle.

Behaving **Misbehaving**

1. Sit quietly when the teacher talks.

2. Make and throw paper planes.

3. Whisper and giggle when the teacher talks.

4. Raise hands to talk.

5. Act rude during story hour.

6. Squirm and make faces.

7. Take turns and share.

8. Throw spitballs at the ceiling.

#357 Literature and Critical Thinking Book 3

MISS NELSON AND MISS SWAMP

How are Miss Nelson and Miss Viola Swamp different? Read the words in the word box. Write each word under the person it describes.

ugly
read stories
kind
snappy voice

sweet voice
wicked
pretty
no stories

Miss Nelson

Miss Viola Swamp

1._____
2._____
3._____
4._____

1._____
2._____
3._____
4._____

62

WELCOME BACK!

The students in Room 207 were very happy to get their teacher back after she had been "gone."

Make believe your teacher has been gone and then comes back.

1. Write a card that tells your teacher how much you missed him or her.
2. Cut it out, fold it down on the center line, and make a picture on the front. Give it to your teacher.

RULES!

1. Make a list of three rules for good classroom behavior.

2. Under each rule, write why the rule is important.

3. Work with a partner. When you are finished, share your rules and reasons with the class.

CLASS RULES

by

_____ *and* _____

Rule 1: _____

    Reason: _____

_____

_____

Rule 2: _____

    Reason: _____

_____

_____

Rule 3: _____

    Reason: _____

_____

TEACHER, TEACHER

1. At the beginning of the story, Miss Nelson's class was the worst-behaved class in school. Why do you think the students in her class misbehaved?

_____

_____

_____

_____

_____

2. When Miss Viola Swamp was the teacher for room 207, the students did **not** misbehave. Why do you think they behaved? _____

_____

_____

3. When Miss Nelson came back to her class, the students behaved beautifully. Why were they so good? _____

_____

_____

4. Do you think they will stay good? _____
   Why? _____

_____

_____

5. What should Miss Nelson do to make sure they don't misbehave horribly again? _____

_____

_____

YOU!

1. Do you ever misbehave in class?____
    Why? _____

2. Do any of the children in your
    room misbehave in class? _____
    Why? _____

3. Keep a record of all behavior
    for one day. Mark a check in the box each time you or a
    classmate does something on the list. Add misbehaviors if
    you need to in the blank boxes at the bottom of the chart.

BEHAVIOR	CHECKS	TOTAL
Throws spitballs		
Tosses paper airplanes		
Does not listen to the teacher when asked to be quiet		
Whispers and giggles while the teacher talks		
Squirms and makes faces		
Is rude during story hour		
Refuses to do lessons		

4. "Grade" your class for this day. Circle your behavior.

    EXCELLENT   **NOT VERY GOOD**
            ALL RIGHT   **TERRIBLE**

5. What did you learn about your class?_____
    _____
    _____

Miss Rumphius

by Barbara Cooney

Alice Rumphius told her grandfather that she would like to do two things in her lifetime - travel to faraway places and live in a house by the sea. Her grandfather added a third thing - "Make the world more beautiful," he told her.

When she grew up, she became a librarian and was called Miss Rumphius. Later, she left her library to travel to faraway places. Miss Rumphius visited tropical islands, snow-covered mountains, jungles, and deserts. But while riding a camel, she hurt her back, making her decide to give up travel and live by the sea.

Miss Rumphius enjoyed her life by the sea. However, she wondered what she could do to fulfill her third goal - to make the world more beautiful. While gazing at the colorful lupines in bloom, she came upon the answer. She scattered lupine seeds about the countryside - five bushels of them.

Soon, the world **was** more beautiful. Miss Rumphius, the Lupine Lady, had achieved what she had set out to do.

FAVORITE FLOWER

Color the flower Miss Rumphius likes best.

DAISY

TULIP

LUPINE

68

SCRAMBLED PICTURES

Color these pictures of things that happen in the story.

Cut each picture out.

Paste the pictures on a piece of paper in story order.

WHAT IS IMPORTANT?

Miss Rumphius wants to do three important things in her life. Do you remember what they are?

Look at these pictures and read the words. Color the IMPORTANT box if the picture is one of the three important things for Miss Rumphius. Next, color the pictures that go along with the boxes.

1) Eat out every day

IMPORTANT

2) Go to faraway places

IMPORTANT

3) Raise kittens

IMPORTANT

4) Live by the sea

IMPORTANT

5) Make world beautiful

IMPORTANT

6) Read books

IMPORTANT

WHY?

Miss Rumphius is doing something in this picture.

What happens because of what she is doing?

Draw your answer in this picture and then color the picture.

#357 Literature and Critical Thinking Book 3

GRANDFATHER AND ALICE?

Make paper bag puppets for Grandfather and Alice (see diagram). Think of some things they would say to each other. **You** act out both parts in front of the class.

GRANDFATHER

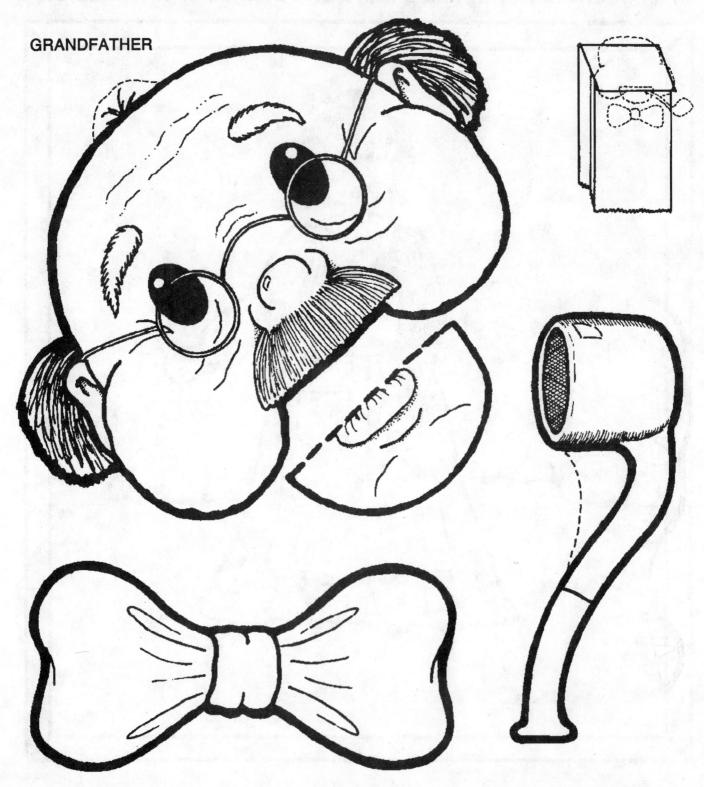

GRANDFATHER AND ALICE?

Make paper bag puppets for Grandfather and Alice (see diagram). Think of some things they would say to each other. **You** act out both parts in front of the class.

ALICE

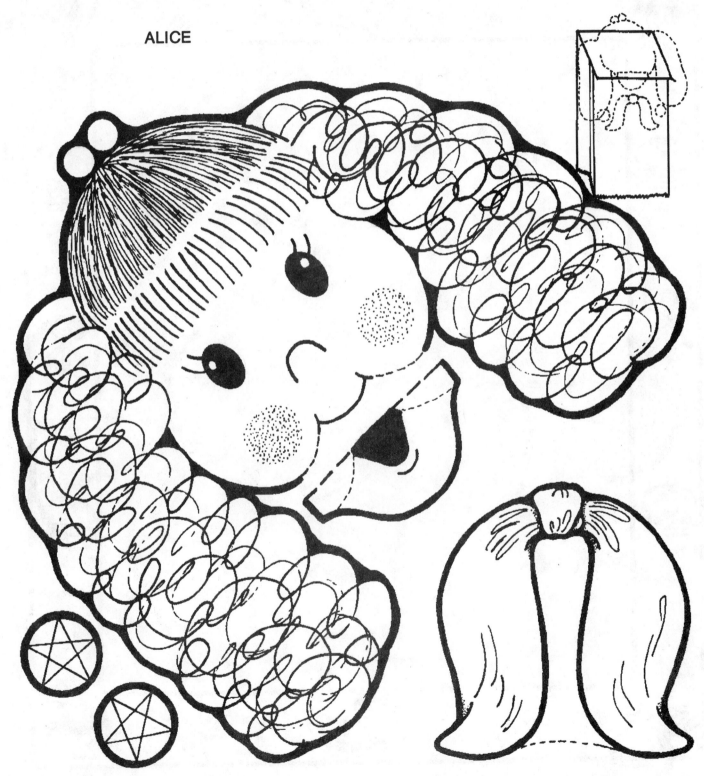

PICNIC SPOT

You and Miss Rumphius are going on a picnic together. Draw a spot for the picnic that you know Miss Rumphius would love.

ME, TOO!

Here are ten things Miss Rumphius does in the story. Color the seashell next to everything you would do, too.

1. Miss Rumphius listens to what her grandfather says.

2. Miss Rumphius works in a library.

3. Miss Rumphius visits a tropical island.

4. Miss Rumphius climbs a snow-covered mountain.

5. Miss Rumphius rides a camel.

6. Miss Rumphius makes friends all over the world.

7. Miss Rumphius lives by the sea.

8. Miss Rumphius plants flower seeds in her yard.

9. Miss Rumphius scatters flower seeds all over town and countryside.

10. Miss Rumphius tells stories to young children.

WHAT IS SHE LIKE?

What kind of person is Miss Rumphius? Is she kind or mean?
Is she scared or brave? Is she happy or sad? Color each
picture that shows what she is like.

KIND MEAN SCARED

BRAVE HAPPY SAD

76

TRAVEL TIME!

Miss Rumphius loves to travel to faraway places. Where should she travel next? **You** plan her trip!

Work in groups of 2 or 3. Make a travel folder to help her. Use encyclopedias, maps, and books for information.

Your travel folder will have 4 pages.

This is page 1 ➞

1. Write the place she is going and your names on the blanks.
2. Color the picture and cut the page out.

Pages 2 and 3 are on the next page.

3. Fill in the blanks on page 2.
4. Draw a map of the place and color Miss Rumphius on page 3.
5. Fold on the broken line.

Page 4 is a picture.

6. Draw a picture on the back of page 3 of Miss Rumphius in the place

A Trip For

Miss Rumphius

to

_____

Planned By

_____
_____
_____

1

she is going (or something she could do there).

7. Paste page 1 on the back of page 2. Draw or paste page 4 on the back of page 3.

　　　　　　　　#357 Literature and Critical Thinking Book 3

TRAVEL TIME!

Things Miss Rumphius should know before she leaves:

1. Name of place: _____

2. Where place is in the world: _____

3. Language people speak there: _____

4. How she will get there: _____

5. Foods eaten in this place: _____

6. Clothes to take: _____

7. Interesting things to do while in this place: _____

8. How long she should stay: _____

2

Map of place:

3

THE LUPINE

FIELD

1. Color this lupine blue, purple, or rose. Then color the leaves green and the stems brown.

3. Cut out the lupine with the box attached.

2. Write your name in the box and an idea you have to make the world more beautiful.

4. Make a class bulletin board of all the lupines. It will look like a field of lupines!

NAME: _____

Something I can do to make the world more beautiful:

_____

_____

APPLESEED MEETS RUMPHIUS

Do you know the story of Johnny Appleseed? He was a man who went around the countryside, planting apple seeds as he traveled. Soon, there were apple trees wherever he walked.

1. How is the story of Johnny Appleseed like the story of Miss Rumphius?

_____

_____

2. Color the things that are the same in both stories.

Johnny Appleseed   Miss Rumphius

3. Do you think Johnny Appleseed would like Miss Rumphius?_____
   Why?_____

4. Do you think Miss Rumphius would like Johnny Appleseed?_____
   Why?_____

GOALS

Miss Rumphius has three goals in her life:
1) To travel to faraway places
2) To live in a house by the sea
3) To make the world more beautiful

1. Do you think it is important to make the world more beautiful? _____

2. Would you like to do any of these things? _____
   Which Ones? _____
   _____

3. Do yo think it is important to make the world more beautiful? _____
   Why? _____
   _____

4. What could you do to make the world more beautiful?
   _____

5. Would it be easy or hard for you to do? _____
   Do you have any special goals for your life like Miss Rumphius has? _____
   What would you like to do in your lifetime? _____
   _____
   _____

6. On the back of this paper, draw yourself doing one of these things.

81

Make Way For Ducklings

by Robert McCloskey

Mr. and Mrs. Mallard looked long and hard for a safe place to have their ducklings. It had to be just right, with no foxes or turtles. They found a lovely spot, the Public Garden in Boston. Complete with water, an island, and a steady source of peanuts, it seemed perfect — until a wildly reckless bicycle rider changed their view. The couldn't lay eggs and raise babies with this danger nearby, so they continued their search.

A small island on the Charles River proved to be a quiet nesting place. The island was near the Public Garden. On the banks of the river walked a kindly police officer, Michael, who loved to feed peanuts to the ducks. Until the ducklings were old enough to migrate to the Public Garden, the island would be home.

Eight ducklings were born to Mr. and Mrs. Mallard. Soon after, Mr. Mallard left to explore the river, setting a Public Garden rendezvous in a week. During that week, Mrs. Mallard taught her babies the many survival skills all ducklings need to learn. At the end of their training period, Mrs. Mallard began the journey to the Public Garden with her ducklings. Her peanut-feeding friend Michael came to her aid, directing traffic and alerting other policemen to help with the migration through the city.

By story's end, Mrs. Mallard and her eight ducklings safely rejoined Mr. Mallard in the Public Garden, glad to finally be home.

HOW MANY?

How many ducklings did Mr. and Mrs. Mallard have? Color them.

STORY ORDER

Color these pictures and cut them out. Paste them in story order on a strip of construction paper.

NOT HERE!

What is happening in this picture? Why don't Mr. and Mrs. Mallard build a nest nearby?_____

_____

_____

Color this picture.

HELPER

Draw a picture of the person who helps **the most** in Mrs. Mallard's trip to the Public Garden with her ducklings.

86

HUMAN, ANIMAL OR THING

Decide if these are human, animal, or thing. Then, write each one in the correct column.

foxes	*Mrs. Mallard*	*turtles*
island	*swan boat*	*Public Garden*
bicycle	*Mr. Mallard*	*river*
Michael	*ducklings*	*peanuts*
policeman	*Clancy*	*car*

HUMAN	ANIMAL	THING
1. _____	1. _____	1. _____
2. _____	2. _____	2. _____
3. _____	3. _____	3. _____
	4. _____	4. _____
	5. _____	5. _____
		6. _____
		7. _____

I SEE . . .

Pretend you are one of the ducklings following Mrs. Mallard on the walk to the Public Garden.

Describe one thing that you see. Remember to see it from a **tiny duckling's eyes**. You may draw a picture or use words. If you use words, make your own lines.

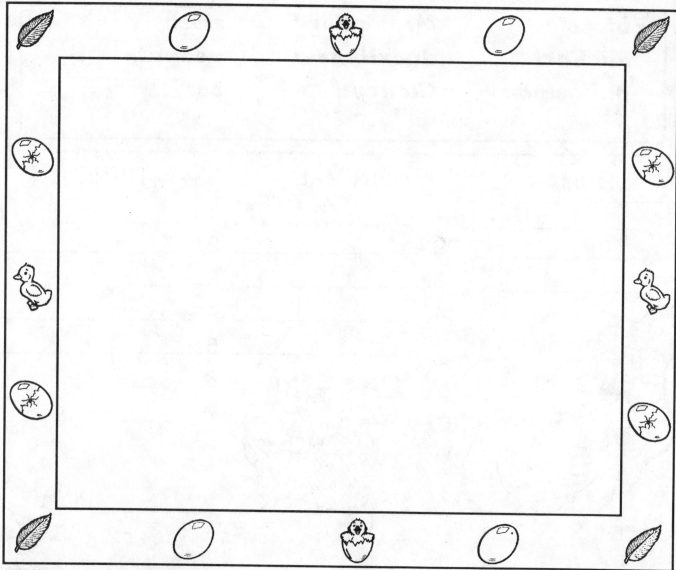

88

MICHAEL SAYS

You met Michael the policeman in **Make Way for Ducklings**. Do you know the type of person he is?

Read these sentences. Write **"YES"** next to the things Michael **might** say. Write **"NO"** next to the things Michael **would not** say.

1. _____ "I wish that boy on this bicycle would chase these ducks away."

2. _____ "I hate to feed the ducks!"

3. _____ "I wonder where the ducks are. I haven't seen them for awhile and I miss them."

4. _____ "There are my little friends, quacking to cross the street."

5. _____ "What stupid ducks — trying to cross the street."

6. _____ "Stop, cars. Let the ducklings cross safely."

7. _____ "Mr. and Mrs. Mallard, I love your new family!"

BELIEVE IT OR NOT!

Look at these pictures of things that happen in the story. If you **believe** that the picture could happen in real life, write ''**I believe this**'' under the picture. If you **do not believe** that the picture could happen in real life, write ''**I do not believe this**'' under the picture.

(This is a 3-page activity)

Page 1

1. Color the duckling.

2. Cut it out.

3. Use paste or glue to attach feathers to the duckling.

4. Put the duckling inside the egg made with pages 2 and 3.

5. Make a class bulletin board of bushes, rocks, grasses, and water. Attach all the eggs to the board.

Teacher: A down pillow is a good source for feathers.

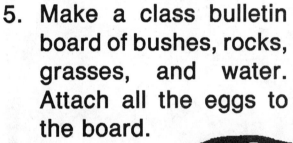

CRACK

(This is a 3-page activity)

Page 2

1. Color the egg shell. Cut the egg out in two pieces. (Cut the egg apart along the dashed line.)

2. Use staples or glue to attach the egg pieces to the egg from the next page.

3. Write your name for the duckling on the top line.

I am a duckling.

My name is

_____

I was made by

_____

4. Write your name on the bottom line.

CRACK

(This is a 3-page activity)

Page 3

1. Cut the egg out. Color the back side of the egg.

2. Use staples or glue to attach the egg shell pieces from page 2.

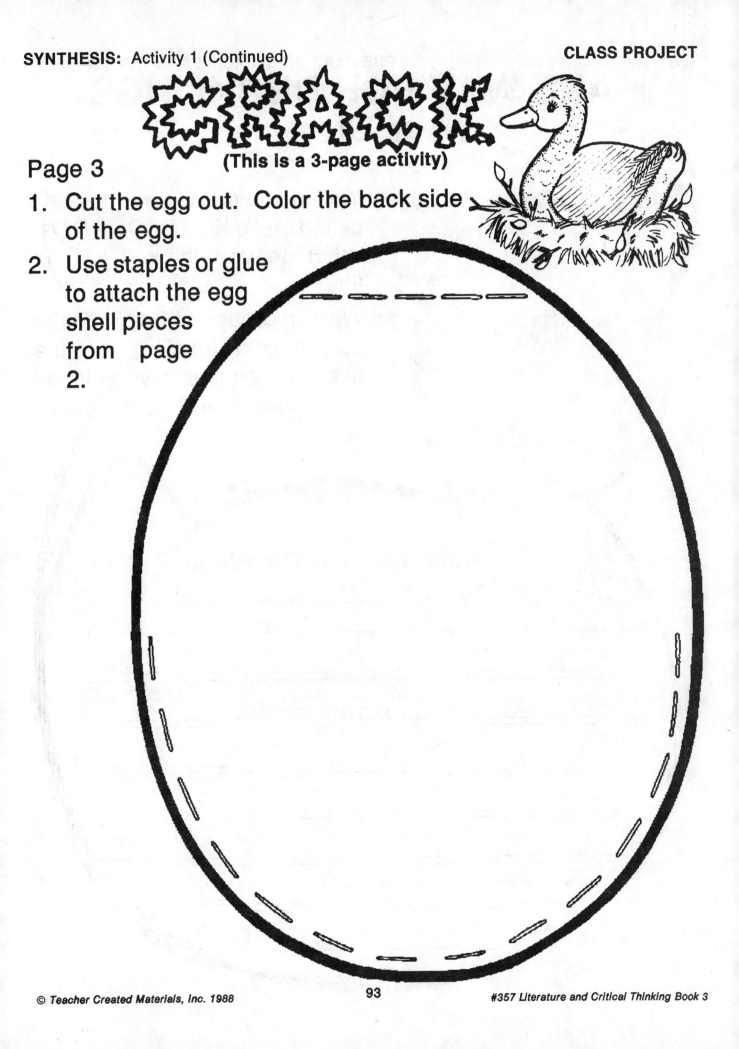

MAKE WAY FOR DUCKLINGS
☆ Your Story ☆

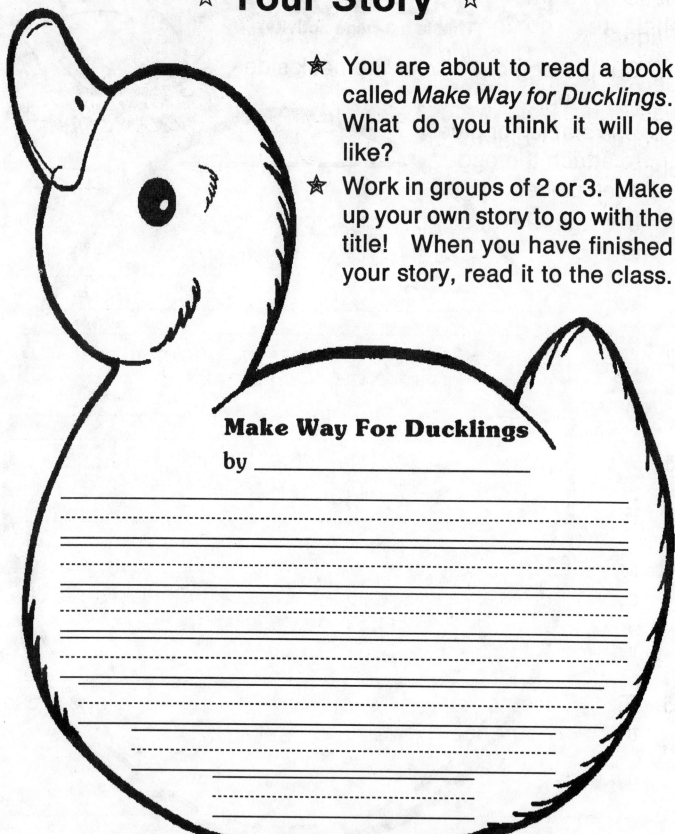

☆ You are about to read a book called *Make Way for Ducklings*. What do you think it will be like?

☆ Work in groups of 2 or 3. Make up your own story to go with the title! When you have finished your story, read it to the class.

Make Way For Ducklings

by _____

JUDGE!

Read what these characters do in *Make Way for Ducklings*. Decide if what they did was right or wrong. Circle and explain your choice.

1. Mrs. Mallard does not want to build her nest near foxes and turtles. **RIGHT**   **WRONG**

   Why? _____

   _____

2. A boy wildly rides his bicycle near the ducks. **RIGHT**   **WRONG**

   Why? _____

   _____

3. A policeman named Michael feeds the ducks peanuts. **RIGHT**   **WRONG**

   Why? _____

   _____

4. Mr. Mallard decides to leave Mrs. Mallard and the new ducklings for a week to see what the rest of the river is like. **RIGHT**   **WRONG**

   Why? _____

   _____

5. Five policemen help Mrs. Mallard and the ducklings cross the busy streets. **RIGHT**   **WRONG**

   Why? _____

   _____

ANSWER KEY

ALEXANDER AND THE TERRIBLE, HORRIBLE, NO GOOD, VERY BAD DAY

K-1   Many to choose from — check story. (K-2 has 12 of them.)

K-2   1) gum 2) skateboard 3) cereal 4) friend 5) dessert 6) cavity 7) mud 8) white 9) lima 10) cat

CORDUROY

K-1   Green

K-2   "Oh, Mommy!" — girl pointing

"Hello!" — night watchman

"I didn't . . ." — Corduroy, one button

"Not today, dear." — mother

"I like you . . ." — girl mending

"You must be a friend." — Corduroy, both buttons

Ap-1   human: Lisa, saleslady, night watchman, Lisa's mother

animal: none (Corduroy is not a real animal)

thing: overalls, mattress, flashlight, button, piggy bank, Corduroy

An-1   could happen: 1, 2, 3 (child could give example of a battery-operated talking bear), 6, 7, 8 (same "battery-operated" example)

couldn't happen: 3 (toy bear couldn't "really" talk), 4, 5, 8 (same reality example)

AMELIA BEDELIA

K-1   Amelia makes a pie.

K-2   Green/cut out in different designs

C-1   Mrs. Rogers: 2, 3, 6

Amelia: 1, 4, 5

C-2   Pie (lemon-meringue)

Ap-1   1) Bill Twill 2) Amy Ramy 3) David Mavid 4) Christopher Histopher 5) Ivan Ryvan 6) Becky Zecky 7) Joe Hoe

8) Mary Parry 9) Lisa Fisa 10) Nicky Kicky

Ap-2   Be sure class is a "critical" audience.

An-2   yes

1) Replace 2) Wipe 3) Close 4) Turn 5) Get

MISS NELSON IS MISSING

K-1   They whispered and giggled.

They made faces.

K-2   Check for appropriateness.

C-1   Miss Nelson is Miss Viola Swamp.

C-2   1) Students misbehave in Miss Nelson's class.

2) Students behave in Miss Viola Swamp's class.

An-1   1) behaving 2) misbehaving 3) misbehaving 4) behaving 5) misbehaving 6) misbehaving 7) behaving 8) misbehaving

An-2   Miss Nelson: 1) read stories 2) kind (pretty) 3) sweet voice 4) pretty (kind)

Miss Viola Swamp: 1) no stories 2) wicked (ugly) 3) snappy voice 4) ugly (wicked)

MISS RUMPHIUS

K-1   Lupine

K-2   1) grandfather & girl 2) librarian 3) climbing a mountain 4) seaside home

C-1   2, 4, 5

C-2   Lupines should be added to the picture.

An-2   kind, brave, happy

MAKE WAY FOR DUCKLINGS

K-1   8

K-2   1) Mr. & Mrs. Mallard flying 2) Mrs. Mallard on nest 3) Mrs. Mallard and ducklings on street walk

4) Mr. & Mrs. Mallard and ducklings swimming together

C-1   Boy on bicycle: smashes eggs and/or ducklings by unsafe riding

C-2   Michael the Policeman

Ap-1   human: Michael, policemen, Clancy

animal: foxes, Mrs. Mallard, Mr. Mallard, ducklings, turtles

thing: island, bicycle, swan boat, Public Garden, river, peanuts, car

An-1   yes: 3, 4, 6, 7

no: 1, 2, 5